DWIGHT D. EISENHOWER

PIVOTAL PRESIDENTS

Profiles in Leadership

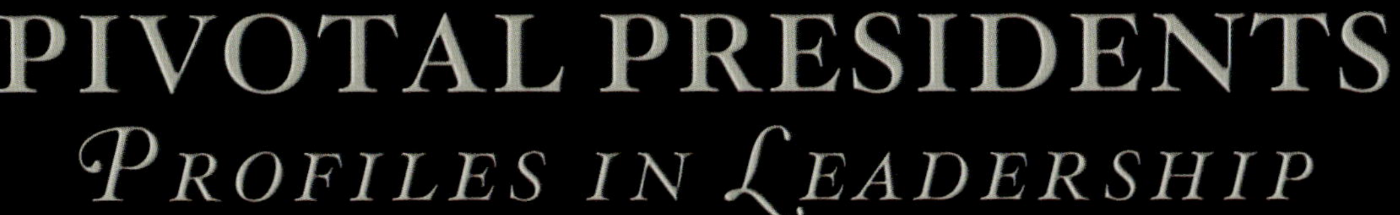

DWIGHT D. EISENHOWER

Edited by Kelly Roscoe

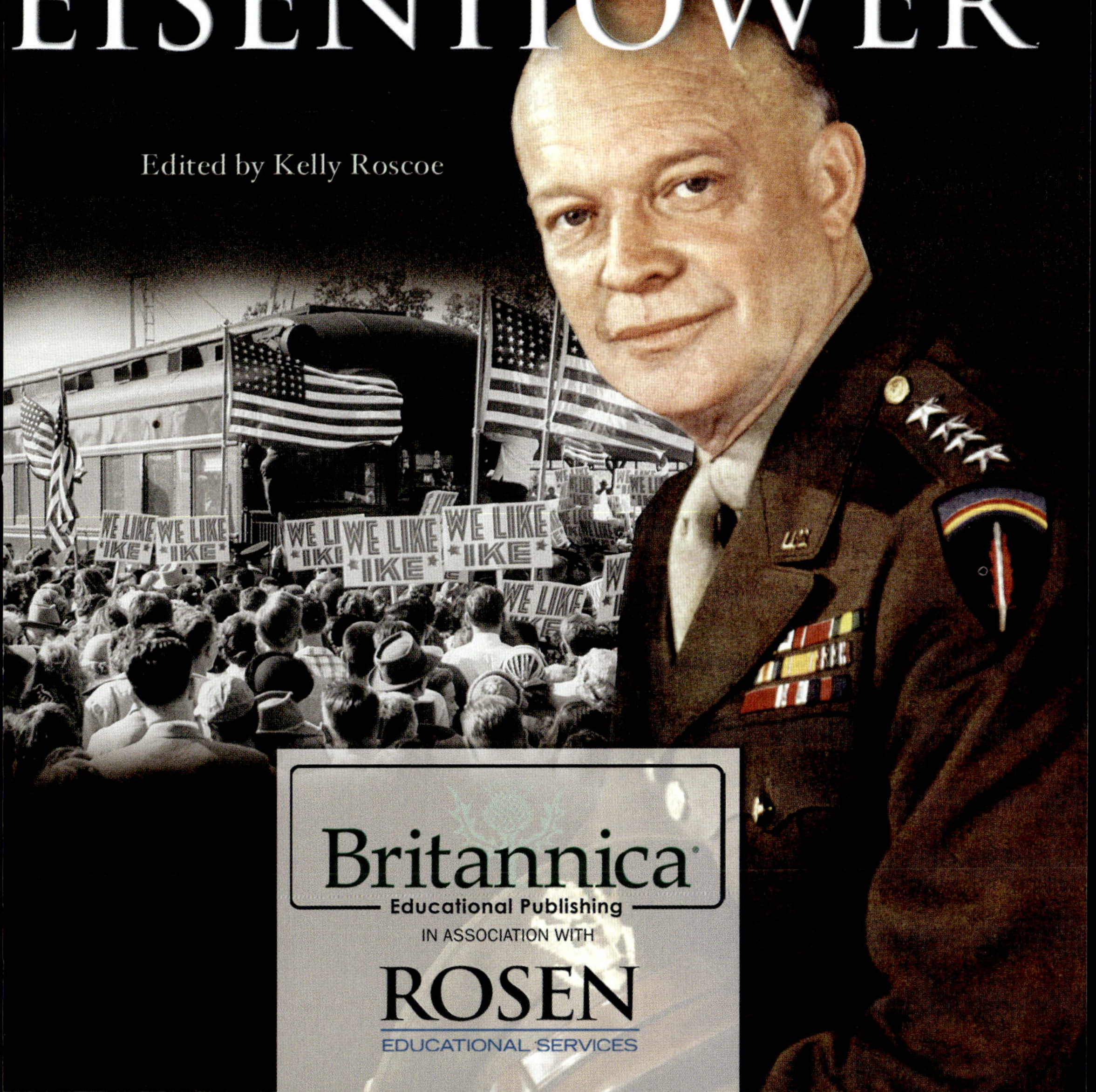

Britannica
Educational Publishing
IN ASSOCIATION WITH
ROSEN
EDUCATIONAL SERVICES

Published in 2017 by Britannica Educational Publishing (a trademark of Encyclopædia Britannica, Inc.) in association with The Rosen Publishing Group, Inc.
29 East 21st Street, New York, NY 10010

Distributed exclusively by Rosen Publishing.
To see additional Britannica Educational Publishing titles, go to rosenpublishing.com.

First Edition

Britannica Educational Publishing
J.E. Luebering: Executive Director, Core Editorial
Anthony L. Green: Editor, Compton's by Britannica

Rosen Publishing
Kelly Roscoe: Editor
Nelson Sá: Art Director
Ellina Litmanovich: Designer
Cindy Reiman: Photography Manager
Bruce Donnola: Photo Researcher

Library of Congress Cataloging-in-Publication Data

Names: Roscoe, Kelly, editor.
Title: Dwight D. Eisenhower / edited by Kelly Roscoe.
Description: First edition. | New York, NY : Britannica Educational Publishing, 2016. | Series: Pivotal presidents: profiles in leadership | Includes bibliographical references and index. | Audience: Grade 7 to 12.
Identifiers: LCCN 2015049686 | ISBN 9781680485240 (library bound : alk. paper)
Subjects: LCSH: Eisenhower, Dwight D. (Dwight David), 1890-1969. | Presidents--United States--Biography. | United States--Politics and government--1953-1961. | Generals--United States--Biography. | World War, 1939-1945--Biography.
Classification: LCC E836 .D8335 2016 | DDC 973.921092--dc23
LC record available at http://lccn.loc.gov/2015049686

Manufactured in China.

Photo credits: Cover, p. 3 (portrait) RDA/Tallandier/Hulton Archive/Getty Images; cover, pp. 3 (background), 38 Ralph Morse/The LIFE Images Collection/Getty Images; cover, pp. 1, 3 (flag) © iStockphoto.com/spxChrome; p. 6 Underwood Archives/Archive Photos/Getty Images; pp. 11, 12, 14, 45 Encyclopædia Britannica, Inc.; p. 17 Hulton Archive/Archive Photos/Getty Images; p. 23 National Archives, Washington, D.C.; p. 25, 44, 65 ©AP Images; p. 27 Popperfoto/Getty Images; p. 29 U.S. Signal Corps/National Archives, Washington, D.C.; p. 33 Library of Congress Prints and Photographs Division; p. 35 Keystone-France/Gamma-Keystone/Getty Images; p. 41 © United Nations /IAEA; p. 47 George Tames/Archive Photos/Getty Images; pp. 49, 54 Carl Iwasaki/The LIFE Images Collection/Getty Images; p. 52 NASA (MSFC-75-SA-4105-2C); p. 56 AFP/Getty Images; 59 Paul Schutzer/The LIFE Images Collection/Getty Images p. 61 Sovfoto/Universal Images Group/Getty Images; p. 64 PhotoQuest/Archive Photos/Getty Images; p. 67 © imac/Alamy Stock Photo; interior pages flag Fedorov Oleksiy/Shutterstock.com.

Table of Contents

INTRODUCTION

As president, Eisenhower used many of the strengths that had served him so well as a general during World War II.

After a long Army career, Dwight D. Eisenhower advanced rapidly through the ranks at the beginning of World War II thanks to his leadership skills and ability to get along with everyone. These same qualities served him well in his second career as a politician and two-term president of the United States.

During World War II Eisenhower became one of the most successful commanders in history. He directed three successful invasions, of North Africa, Italy, and France, that turned the tide of the war and hastened the Allies' victory on the European front. After the war the five-star general added to his military reputation through his work as Army chief of staff. Later he became the first head of the armies of the North Atlantic Treaty Organization (NATO). Turning to politics in 1952, Eisenhower proved to be a successful commander in that field also. After winning the Republican nomination for president, he overwhelmingly defeated the Democratic candidate, Adlai E. Stevenson. He thus became the 34th president of the United States and the first Republican president in 20 years.

During Eisenhower's first term as president, 1953–57, the Korean War ended and the United States went on to achieve the greatest prosperity in its history up to that time. Eisenhower advocated for public works projects and reduced government spending.

In 1956 the Republican Party unanimously renominated Eisenhower for the presidency. Campaigning on a platform of "peace and prosperity," Eisenhower decisively defeated the same Democratic opponent, Stevenson. He received 457 electoral votes to Stevenson's 73.

Eisenhower's second term was marked by tensions related to the developing civil rights movement. In 1954 the Supreme Court, led by Eisenhower's choice for chief justice, Earl Warren, had declared that separate schools for black and white students were unconstitutional. Three years later the governor of Arkansas called in the National Guard to prevent black students from attending an all-white high school in Little Rock. Eisenhower sent federal troops to protect the students. In the same year Congress passed the first civil rights act since the end of Reconstruction.

Eisenhower faced other challenges abroad, including the Suez crisis in the Middle East and the Soviet Union's successful launch of the first artificial satellite, Sputnik I. He aimed to reduce tension in the Cold War and invited Soviet premier Nikita Khrushchev to visit the United States in 1959. Eisenhower himself embarked on several goodwill tours around the world in his final years as president.

In his Farewell Address, Eisenhower warned that the armaments industry, though necessary for the nation's security, could endanger the American democratic process. Despite this warning, the Cold War would only intensify during the administration of his successor, John F. Kennedy. However, during his eight years as president, Eisenhower had proved himself to be more than just a strong leader on the battlefield. As commander in chief and head of state, he presided over a nation that was gaining in prosperity even as it grappled with issues of security and civil rights.

CHAPTER 1

Early Life and Military Career

The future president was born in 1890. Most published sources refer to his birth name as David Dwight Eisenhower, which is also how it appears in the family Bible. Two biographers of Eisenhower, Stephen Ambrose and Carlo D'Este, believe that his mother reversed his given names to Dwight David shortly after his birth. She reportedly did this partly because she did not like nicknames and thought that Dwight could never be shortened and partly because she thought it would be confusing to have a son with the same name as his father, David.

BOYHOOD IN KANSAS

The name Eisenhower comes from German words meaning a kind of ironworker. The president's father, David Eisenhower, was descended from German immigrants who had settled in Pennsylvania during the 1730s. In 1878 the family moved to Abilene, Kansas. The president's mother, Ida Elizabeth (Stover) Eisenhower, had moved from Virginia to Kansas in 1883.

Eisenhower's parents met at a United Brethren school in Lecompton, Kansas. They married in 1885. A few years later David Eisenhower moved his family from Abilene to Denison, Texas. Dwight was born there on October 14, 1890. He was the third of his parents' seven sons, one of whom died of diphtheria

Eisenhower, pictured with his brothers, lived in this home in Abilene, Kansas, from 1892 until he left for West Point in 1911.

when he was 10 months old. Two years after Dwight's birth the family returned to Abilene.

The future president, with his brothers Arthur, Edgar, Roy, Earl, and Milton, grew up on the old homestead of his grandfather Jacob Eisenhower. In 1947 this home became a national shrine. Family souvenirs and papers are housed in the Eisenhower Presidential Museum, opened in Abilene in 1954. David worked in a creamery, and the family was poor. Dwight and his brothers were introduced to hard work and a strong religious tradition at an early age.

During his school days young Dwight was

Major Dwight D. Eisenhower *(standing, third from left)* **with his brothers and his parents in about 1935.**

usually called Ike by his friends. The nickname stayed with him throughout his life. Ike's favorite school subjects were English, history, and geometry, but he took only a moderate interest in his studies. Even as an adult Eisenhower did not enjoy the company of scholars. He much preferred sports and excelled at both baseball and football.

Early Military Career and Marriage

Ike graduated from Abilene High School in 1909. For the next two years he worked in a creamery to help pay Edgar's expenses at college. In 1911 he took the entrance examination for the Military Academy at West Point. His mother, who was a pacifist, cried when she found out Ike wanted to join the military. Though he ranked second in the tests, he obtained the appointment when the top candidate failed to pass the physical examination.

The young cadet was a promising halfback on the academy football team but had to give up the game after injuring his knee. Eisenhower graduated from West Point in 1915 and was

Eisenhower as a graduate of the U.S. Military Academy at West Point, New York, 1915.

commissioned a second lieutenant of infantry. He ranked 61st in a class of 168 students, 59 of whom would go on to become generals.

Eisenhower was assigned to the 19th Infantry Regiment at Fort Sam Houston, Texas. In nearby San Antonio he met Mamie Doud of Denver. He gave her a miniature of his West Point class ring (amethyst set in gold) to mark their engagement on Valentine's Day in 1916. Despite her father's worries that the life of a military wife would be too difficult, they married on July 1, 1916, at the Douds' Denver home. That same day Eisenhower was promoted to first lieutenant.

The couple began married life in military housing in San Antonio. As Dwight's career took them all over the world, Mamie ran many different homes, often with little money, and by the time she moved into the White House she estimated that she had unpacked at least 27 times. Wherever the military led them, the Eisenhowers had the tradition of hosting a weekly buffet, often followed by Mamie playing the piano. The Eisenhowers had two sons: Doud Dwight, born in 1917, who died of scarlet fever in 1921, and John Sheldon Doud, born in 1922. John also became an officer in the Army.

Mamie Eisenhower

Mamie Geneva Doud was born on November 14, 1896, in Boone, Iowa. When she was seven, her father had accumulated enough wealth to retire, and the family moved to Denver, Colorado. Mamie attended public schools, followed by a year of finishing school. The family wintered in San Antonio, Texas, and it was there in October 1915 that Mamie met Eisenhower, a young Army lieutenant six years her senior.

Whether at a military post in the jungles of Panama or at the White House, Mamie Eisenhower believed her duty was to be supportive of her husband and to create a happy home for him. In an era when a strong family unit was believed to be a defense against communism, the First Lady became a role model. In her feminine (often pink) dresses and stylish haircut with her trademark bangs, she took obvious delight in being beside her husband and serving as his official hostess.

Immensely popular with crowds and comfortable with important people, Mamie thrived on her duties as first lady, and she was known for gracious entertaining. The diplomacy of the postwar years and the development of air travel enabled the Eisenhowers to entertain an unprecedented number of heads of state and leaders of foreign governments. White House employees reported that Mamie supervised them closely, always on the lookout for lapses. She disliked giving speeches, and her press conferences consisted of listing social activities. Determinedly nonpartisan, Mamie published an article in *Good Housekeeping* in 1952 that she titled, "Vote for My Husband or for Governor Stevenson, but Please Vote."

Mamie's balance problem prompted some rumors of alcoholism. When Eisenhower was questioned on the

continued on page 18

Mamie Eisenhower in about 1950.

continued from page 16

subject in 1952, he replied that he was aware that "the story has gone around" but that she "had not had a drink for something like 18 months." Historians have generally concluded that, at least during her years in the White House, her balance problem stemmed more from an inner ear disease than from excessive drinking.

After Eisenhower suffered a major heart attack in 1955, Mamie had mixed emotions on whether or not he should seek a second term. Although she feared for his health, she also worried that retirement might be deadly for him.

After leaving the White House in January 1961, the couple moved to a farm they had purchased near Gettysburg, Pennsylvania, after Eisenhower had become president of Columbia University in the late 1940s. Mamie survived her husband by 10 years, dying on November 1, 1979, at the Walter Reed Army Medical Center in Washington, D.C. She is buried beside him in Abilene, Kansas, in a chapel on the grounds of the Eisenhower Presidential Library.

Soon after the United States entered World War I Eisenhower was promoted to captain. He later received the temporary rank of major and then lieutenant colonel. The war ended one day before he was to sail for France. For his work in organizing a tank corps he was awarded the Distinguished

Service Medal, his highest Army decoration. (Two oak leaf clusters were added to this medal in World War II. He received the Navy Distinguished Service Medal in 1947.)

After World War I Eisenhower was returned to the rank of captain but was soon promoted to major. In the years that followed he had assignments in the United States, the Panama Canal Zone, and Europe. In 1926 he graduated first in his class at the Command and General Staff School. His administrative abilities earned him an executive post in Washington, D.C., from 1929 to 1933. When General Douglas MacArthur became military adviser to the Philippines in 1935, Eisenhower became his assistant. Promoted to lieutenant colonel in 1936, he learned to fly and trained Filipino pilots.

Chapter 2

World War II

Eisenhower returned to the United States in 1940, shortly after Germany's invasion of Poland began the European phase of World War II. After a long Army career in relatively obscure positions, he advanced rapidly because of his knowledge of military strategy as well as his ability to get along with others. Men from a wide variety of backgrounds, impressed by his friendliness, humility, and persistent optimism, liked and trusted him. A phrase that later became one of the most famous campaign slogans in American history seemed to reflect the impression of everyone who met him: "I like Ike!"

North Africa and Italy

When the United States entered World War II in December 1941, Army Chief of Staff General George C. Marshall appointed Eisenhower to the Army's war plans division in Washington, D.C., where he prepared strategy for an Allied invasion of Europe. This plan was known as Operation Roundup. However, the operation was postponed when the British persuaded the Americans to invade North Africa first. The Allied invasion of Europe would not take place until June 1944. In the meantime, Eisenhower played a key role in the Allied operations in both North Africa and Italy.

Eisenhower had been made a brigadier general in September 1941 and was promoted to major general in March 1942. He was also named head of the operations division of the War Department. In June Marshall selected him over 366 senior officers to be commander of U.S. troops in Europe. The next month Marshall promoted Eisenhower again, to lieutenant general, and appointed him to take over planning for the invasion of North Africa. In this position Eisenhower showed great talent for combining officers of different countries into a single team. He also proved he knew how to solve both military and political problems on an international scale.

Eisenhower commanded the U.S. forces in the invasion of North Africa, known as Operation Torch, on November 8, 1942. In the first major Allied offensive of the war, British and Americans troops landed at Algiers, Oran, and Casablanca. The invaders met little resistance and quickly drove inland. On November 15 the French in Africa joined the Allies. Eisenhower's decision to work during the campaign with the French admiral François Darlan, who had collaborated with the Germans, aroused a storm of protest from the Allies, but President Franklin D. Roosevelt defended his action. In February 1943 he was promoted to four-star general.

American forces met their first defeat at the hands of the Germans in the Battle of Kasserine Pass (February 14–25, 1943). They rallied, however, to push through Tunisia. On April 7 U.S. troops met the

British 8th Army as it advanced from the east. The Allies forced 250,000 Germans and Italians to surrender near Cape Bon on May 12, successfully completing Operation Torch.

Allied troops landing on a beach near Algiers during Operation Torch, November 8, 1942.

Also in 1943, Eisenhower directed the invasion of Italy, an amphibious attack across the Mediterranean that started with the invasion of Sicily in July. On July 25 Benito Mussolini was forced to resign as premier of Italy. The British 8th Army invaded southern Italy on September 3, and Mussolini's successor, Pietro Badoglio, surrendered its armed forces unconditionally on September 8. This took Italy out of the war, but the Germans, under Field Marshal Albert Kesselring, continued to fight. The Allies were forced to battle their way up the Italian mainland throughout the fall and early winter of 1943. Eventually Rome fell to the Allies on June 4, 1944.

D-Day

In December 1943 Eisenhower was appointed supreme commander of the Allied Expeditionary Forces, placing him in charge of the plan to invade France by crossing the English Channel. The next month he was in London making preparations for the massive thrust into Europe. Operation Overlord, as the invasion was known, called for three divisions to land in Normandy, with two brigades to be air-dropped. Another 11 divisions

Eisenhower *(seated, center)* and other top commanders of the Allied Expeditionary Force at their headquarters in London in February 1944.

were to be landed within the first two weeks through two artificial harbors that would be towed across the English Channel. Once a foothold had been established, 100 additional divisions were to be assembled in France for a final assault on Germany.

May 1944 had been chosen as the time for the invasion. Difficulties in assembling landing craft forced a postponement until June, and Eisenhower fixed June 5 as the launch date. As the day approached and troops began to embark for the crossing, bad weather set in, threatening dangerous landing conditions. The invasion was postponed for 24 hours, requiring that some ships already at sea be recalled. On the morning of June 5, however, Eisenhower was assured of a break in the weather the following day, and he gave the order to launch the Normandy Invasion, the largest amphibious attack in history. Within hours, an armada of 3,000 landing craft, 2,500 other ships, and 500 naval vessels began to leave English ports. That night 822 aircraft, carrying parachutists or towing gliders, roared overhead to the Normandy landing zones. They were a fraction of the air armada of 13,000 aircraft that would support the D-Day landing.

American troops land in France on D-Day, June 6, 1944.

The airborne troops arrived first, and their landings were a heartening success. When the seaborne units began to land about 6:30 AM on June 6, the British and Canadians on Gold, Juno, and Sword beaches overcame light opposition. So did the Americans at Utah Beach. The U.S. division at Omaha Beach, however, confronted German machine gunners as the troops waded ashore, and the landing threatened to fail. Only dedicated local leadership eventually got the troops inland—though at a cost of more than 2,000 casualties.

Meanwhile, the German high command began to respond. German dictator Adolf Hitler was initially unwilling to release the armored divisions for a counterattack. When Hitler relented after midday, the German tanks drove into the gap between British and Canadian divisions at Sword Beach and Juno Beach and almost reached the sea. Had they done so, the Allied landings might have failed. Fierce resistance by British antitank gunners turned the tide in late evening. It took the Allies six days of extensive fighting to gain control of the entire beachhead.

As the Allies attempted to push inland into France, they encountered fierce German resistance and counterattacks. Germany's bitter defense, however, was costing them men and equipment that could not be replaced. In addition, the German high command was disintegrating.

German prisoners are led past the rangers' command post on Pointe du Hoc on D-Day plus 2, June 8, 1944.

Eisenhower and the Autobahn

Germany began building autobahns, modern express highways for cars, in the early 1930s. More were designed under the direction of Hitler precisely for the purpose of speeding the movement of military transport. This network of highways helped the Germans in their blitzkrieg tactics in the early years of World War II, but the Allies found it equally advantageous as they pushed through France and Germany after the D-Day landing.

Eisenhower admired how easy it was to cross terrain on the autobahn, especially compared to the highways in the United States. In 1919 he had participated in the Transcontinental Motor Convoy, an Army project to determine if motor vehicles, which had only recently begun to be used in combat, could withstand a long trip. The convoy traveled along the Lincoln Highway from New York City to San Francisco, California. However, along much of the route, the roads were not paved, and the bridges were not sturdy enough for heavy military vehicles.

Eisenhower's experiences traveling in Germany and the United States inspired him to improve roads in the United States as president. In an address to Congress on February 22, 1955, he said, "Together, the uniting forces of our communication and transportation systems are dynamic elements in the very name we bear—United States. Without them, we would be a mere alliance of many separate parts." He also pointed out that an interconnected system of well-maintained roads would

reduce automobile accidents and injuries, as well as make it easier to mobilize the military and evacuate the population in case of an atomic attack or other emergency. The following year, he secured passage of the Federal Aid Highway Act, which established the Interstate Highway System.

By late July 1944, American forces staged a devastating air attack on the German forces. On August 16, Hitler gave permission for a withdrawal from Normandy. Within the next few days, German troops were able to break through a gap between American and British troops. While the Germans fled across the Seine River and retreated back across northern France into Belgium, French Resistance forces in Paris rose against what remained of the German garrison there on August 19. Troops arrived on August 24 to liberate the city. The next morning the German commander of Paris surrendered to the French Resistance.

Liberation had come at a high cost: the Allies counted more than 200,000 dead, wounded, and missing, whereas the German numbers rose to more than

300,000. French civilian losses numbered more than 12,000. Still, the Normandy campaign had been a stunning success. By early September 1944, all but a fraction of France had been liberated. The U.S., British, and Canadian forces had occupied Belgium and part of the Netherlands and had reached the German frontier. They had, however, outrun their logistical support and lacked the strength to launch a final offensive. The coming winter would see much hard fighting before the German army in the west was finally beaten.

After winning the Battle of the Bulge—a fierce German counterattack in the Ardennes in December—the Allies crossed the Rhine River on March 7, 1945. Germany surrendered on May 7, ending the war in Europe. Eisenhower was criticized, then and later, for allowing the Russians to capture the enemy capital of Berlin. However, he and others defended his actions on several grounds: the Russians were closer, had more troops, and had been promised Berlin at the Yalta Conference of February 1945. Meanwhile, in December 1944, Eisenhower had received the highest U.S. military rank, five-star general.

Eisenhower gives orders to paratroopers preparing for the Normandy Invasion, launched on D-Day, June 6, 1944.

Postwar Positions

Eisenhower was given a hero's welcome upon returning to the United States for a visit in June 1945, but in November his intended retirement was delayed when President Harry S. Truman named him to replace Marshall as chief of staff. For more than two years Eisenhower directed demobilization of the wartime army and worked to unify the armed services under a centralized command. In May 1948 he left active duty the most popular and respected soldier in the United States and became president of Columbia University in New York City. His book *Crusade in Europe*, published that fall, made him a wealthy man.

Eisenhower's brief career as an academic administrator was not especially successful. His technical education and military experience prepared him poorly for the post. In 1949 he obtained leave from Columbia to preside over the joint chiefs of staff during the unification of the armed forces that occurred when the War Department was changed to the Defense Department. In the fall of 1950 President Truman asked him to become supreme commander of the North Atlantic Treaty Organization (NATO), and in early 1951 he flew to Paris to assume his new position.

Eisenhower presents his defense plans at a NATO conference in Rome in November 1951.

NATO is a political and military alliance between the United States, Canada, and numerous European countries. The 12 founding member nations signed the North Atlantic Treaty on April 4, 1949, as a defense against the Soviet Union and its eastern European allies. In Article 5, the heart of the treaty, the member nations agreed that "an armed attack against one or more of them in Europe or North America shall be considered an attack against them all." For the next 15 months after his appointment Eisenhower devoted himself to the task of creating a united military organization in western Europe to be a defense against the possibility of communist aggression. This success increased his already high military and political standing. It also established the precedent that the military leader of NATO would be American, while the political leader would be European.

CHAPTER 3

First Term of Presidency

During his Army career Eisenhower had taken no part in politics and there was some uncertainty as to which party he favored. Early in 1952, however, he revealed publicly that he had always been a Republican. The general also said that he would run for president if he received a "clear-cut call to political duty." Several Republican leaders then entered his name in various state presidential primaries.

In early election contests Eisenhower showed great political strength in New Hampshire, Minnesota, and Nebraska. Recognizing his rising popularity, he resigned from the NATO command and retired from active duty with the Army. He then opened a vigorous campaign for the Republican presidential nomination with a speech in Abilene, Kansas, in June.

NOMINATION AND ELECTION

As a political campaigner Eisenhower was an immediate success. His expressive face and warm sincerity contributed much to his effectiveness as a public speaker. At the Republican convention in Chicago he won the nomination on the first ballot in a close

Supporters wave "We Like Ike" signs at an Eisenhower campaign event in 1952.

race with Senator Robert Taft of Ohio. Senator Richard Nixon, a conservative from California, was selected as the nominee for vice president to balance the ticket ideologically and geographically.

Eisenhower's leadership and great personal charm united all factions of the Republican Party behind his candidacy. Throughout the campaign he called for a firm, middle-of-the-road policy in both foreign and domestic affairs. In an effort to find a solution to the stalemated Korean War he dramatically promised: "I shall go to Korea."

On November 4, 1952, Dwight Eisenhower was elected president by a landslide. He received almost 34 million popular votes, until that time the greatest number ever given a political candidate in the United States. His 442 electoral votes came from 39 states, including such traditionally Democratic states as Florida, Texas, and Virginia. His opponent, Adlai E. Stevenson, had a popular vote of about 27 million and an electoral vote of 89.

The general's sweeping victory helped his party to win control of Congress, although the Republican majority in both houses was small. Because the Republican margin was so slight, and because many right-wing Republicans in Congress disagreed with his policies,

Eisenhower would increasingly depend upon Democrats to realize his objectives.

Immediately after taking office on January 20, 1953, Eisenhower made clear his intentions to work for world peace. He pledged the United States to a constant search for an honorable settlement of international problems. He also came to office having promised to end the Korean War, hold the line on government spending, balance the budget, abolish inflation, and reform the Republican Party.

Cold War

Foreign affairs—particularly the growing Cold War rivalry between the United States and the Soviet Union—drew much of Eisenhower's attention. The Korean War was a key conflict in the early years of the Cold War. It had begun in 1950 when communist North Korea, backed by the Soviets, invaded South Korea, a democracy supported by the United States.

Four weeks into his presidency, Eisenhower honored his boldest campaign promise by making a special trip to Korea. In a closely guarded visit he toured the battlefront, studying the possibilities of an honorable peace settlement. In July 1953 the president formally announced the signing of a truce. He warned, however, that the United States must remain on guard against other acts of communist aggression. This warning was underscored in August when the Soviet Union revealed that it had developed a hydrogen bomb.

Eisenhower's "Atoms for Peace" speech to the United Nations in 1953 called for curbing the global nuclear arms race.

The increasing threat of communist expansion in the Far East led to a meeting of eight countries in Manila, Philippines. In September 1954 these countries formed the Southeast Asia Treaty Organization (SEATO) for the collective defense of the area. Member countries were the United States, Australia, France, Great Britain, New Zealand, Pakistan, the Philippines, and Thailand.

In an effort to ease world tensions, the heads of the Big Four powers—the United States, Great Britain, France, and the Soviet Union—met in Geneva, Switzerland, in July 1955. Eisenhower introduced his "open skies" proposal, by which the United States and the Soviet Union would permit continuous air inspection of each other's military installations. It was welcomed by world opinion but was rejected by the Soviet Union. Hostile feelings continued between the Soviets and the West.

Domestic Policy

In domestic affairs Eisenhower was generally conservative. He advocated for reduced taxes, balanced budgets, and a decrease in government control over the economy. One of his first acts was to lift the ceiling imposed on wages in 1951. Then price controls were either removed or allowed to expire. To bring the budget near balance Eisenhower helped block some tax cuts and ordered federal spending reduced. He also called for the return of certain federal responsibilities to the states.

In 1954 Congress reduced excise taxes by about $1 billion a year. Congress also voted for the most comprehensive tax revision in 75 years. This measure decreased national revenue by another $1.3 billion. Still, taxes remained fairly high and defense spending decreased, allowing Eisenhower to avoid serious deficits, stop inflation, and encourage economic growth. Americans as a whole were more prosperous than they had ever been before.

Eisenhower also supported public works and continued most of the social reforms begun under the Democratic presidents who came before him, Franklin D. Roosevelt and Harry S. Truman. In 1954 Congress authorized the United States to join Canada in constructing the St. Lawrence Seaway, a project recommended by every president since Warren G. Harding in the 1920s. Two years later Congress approved the Interstate Highway System, Eisenhower's pet project and the largest public works program in history. The minimum wage was increased to $1 per hour, and amendments to the Social Security Act in 1954 and 1956 extended benefits

This map of the Interstate Highway System from 1966 showed the progress of Eisenhower's pet public works project.

to millions not previously covered. In 1953 the Department of Health, Education, and Welfare was created and given Cabinet rank.

The right wing of the Republican Party clashed with Eisenhower more often than the Democrats did during his first term. The biggest challenge was Republican Senator Joseph McCarthy of Wisconsin, who was investigating charges of communist influence in the U.S. government. Many people thought McCarthy's tactics (labeled "McCarthyism") were a necessary part of his anticommunist investigations. Others charged that McCarthy violated democratic principles.

Privately Eisenhower expressed his distaste for the senator. At times, however, he seemed to encourage McCarthy's attacks. With Eisenhower's approval, Congress passed a law designed to outlaw the American Communist Party. When McCarthy began to investigate the Eisenhower Administration and the Army, however, an investigation of McCarthy's own activities was begun. Late in 1954 the Senate, with Eisenhower playing a behind-the-scenes role, voted to condemn McCarthy for his conduct. McCarthy soon lost all influence.

Senator Joseph McCarthy testifies before a Senate subcommittee on elections and rules in an effort to link fellow senator William Benton to communism.

McCarthyism and the Politics of Fear

President Eisenhower, like many others in the government, disapproved of Senator Joseph McCarthy's methods of attacking suspected communists without evidence. Still, Eisenhower was reluctant to criticize McCarthy publicly. He believed that there was nothing to be gained from attacking individuals in the public arena, and that to do so would damage his prestige as president. However, his silence on the issue led some people to believe that he approved of McCarthy.

In a letter to the governor of Indiana on March 26, 1954, Eisenhower explained why he had not spoken out:

> *Nevertheless, I think that were I to stand up in public and label him [McCarthy] with derogatory titles, I would make a serious error. I still feel that such an attempt would advertise him still more. It would make the Presidency ridiculous and so, in the long run, make the citizens of our country very unhappy indeed.*

Rather than give McCarthy even more of the public attention he craved, Eisenhower encouraged Republican senators to censure McCarthy, which helped discredit the senator. His dangerous accusations had sparked blacklisting in Hollywood and ruined the reputations and careers of many entertainers, politicians, and scholars. McCarthy's witch hunt, the claims of which were never substantiated, is now considered a frightening example of the effectiveness of fear tactics.

In military policy, Eisenhower reduced the size of the Army and Navy while increasing spending on the Air Force. In 1954 he signed a bill establishing an Air Force Academy, similar to the Army's West Point and the Navy's Annapolis. Interested primarily in deterring a nuclear attack, Eisenhower promoted the development of nuclear weapons and long-range missiles.

Two Supreme Court justices died during Eisenhower's first term, requiring the president to make two appointments. In 1953 he named Governor Earl Warren of California as chief justice to succeed Frederick M. Vinson. In 1955 Eisenhower

Earl Warren's tenure as chief justice of the Supreme Court included landmark decisions on race relations and criminal procedure.

chose Judge John Marshall Harlan of New York to replace Justice Robert H. Jackson.

In the 1954 midterm elections, the Democrats narrowly won control of both houses of Congress. The results seemed to indicate a dissatisfaction with the Republican Party in general rather than with the president himself. Many political observers believed that only Eisenhower's elaborate campaigning prevented an even larger Democratic victory. In addition, a public opinion poll revealed that more than two thirds of all the voters thought the president was doing a good job.

Reelection

In September 1955 Eisenhower suffered a heart attack while on vacation in Denver, Colorado. He made a steady recovery and after seven weeks was released from the hospital. After additional rest he resumed his duties in Washington, D.C.

After the president's heart attack there was much uncertainty about whether he would seek another term in office. This speculation ended in February 1956, when Eisenhower announced his candidacy for reelection. He told the voters that his health was good enough to carry on his duties for an additional four years. He remained determined to run despite an intestinal disorder that necessitated an operation in June 1956.

In the election campaign, in which his opponent was again Adlai E. Stevenson of Illinois, Eisenhower stressed his moderate approach to problems. He was reelected by the largest margin achieved by any Republican president up to that time. The Democrats, however, retained control of both houses of Congress.

Eisenhower leaves the hospital in Denver in November 1955.

CHAPTER 4

Second Term of Presidency

In his second term Eisenhower faced serious problems abroad and at home. A chief trouble spot abroad was the Middle East, which was affected by Cold War tensions. Domestic issues included the ongoing civil rights struggle and an economic recession.

NATIONAL DEFENSE AND THE SPACE RACE

The 1956 election campaign had been complicated by a crisis in the Middle East over Egypt's seizure of the Suez Canal. Great Britain, France, and Israel responded by attacking Egypt, which was supported by the Soviet Union. The crisis prompted Eisenhower to issue a policy that came to be called the Eisenhower Doctrine. He pledged to send military and economic aid to any Middle Eastern country requesting assistance against communist aggression. The plan was a continuation of the containment policy adopted in the 1940s by the Truman Administration, which was designed to thwart the Soviet Union's expansionist goals. Congress adopted the Eisenhower Doctrine in March 1957.

In October and November 1957 the Soviet Union launched the first two artificial Earth satellites, Sputniks I and II. The Soviet Union also said it had successfully developed an intercontinental ballistic missile. Eisenhower then made a series of talks to reassure the country regarding national security. In December 1957 representatives of the North Atlantic Treaty Organization agreed to arm western Europe with U.S. nuclear missiles.

Many Americans, stunned by the Soviet achievement with Sputnik, feared that the United States had fallen behind its rival in military and space technology, and they blamed Eisenhower. The president responded by boosting space research, and in January 1958

The launch of U.S. satellite Explorer 1 at Cape Canaveral, Florida, on January 31, 1958.

Army scientists put a U.S. satellite, Explorer I, into orbit. In March Navy scientists also launched a satellite, Vanguard I. The Air Force launched an Atlas intercontinental ballistic missile in August.

Eisenhower asked Congress to create a civilian national aeronautics and space agency to administer the country's nonmilitary space research and exploration projects. The new National Aeronautics and Space Administration (NASA) was established in July 1958. Military space activities remained with the Defense Department.

The president also introduced a major change in the organization of the Defense Department. The plan merged operational Army, Navy, and Air Force units under unified commands. The commanders reported directly to the secretary of defense. The reorganization gave the defense secretary greater control over strategic planning and military operations.

Civil Rights

During Eisenhower's second term, race became a central national concern for the first time since the Reconstruction period following the Civil War. Some civil rights advances had been made in recent years. In the landmark case *Brown* v. *Board of Education* (1954) the Supreme Court had ruled that racial segregation in public schools was unconstitutional. This nullified the doctrine of "separate-but-equal" facilities. The decision was met with great hostility in the South, but it was followed by a chain of rulings and orders that also limited discrimination. In 1955 Martin Luther King, Jr., led a boycott of segregated buses in Montgomery, Alabama, giving rise to the nonviolent civil rights movement.

Children whose parents filed the *Brown* v. *Board of Education* lawsuit, shown in 1953. Linda Brown, whose parents were the lead plaintiffs, is third from left.

Neither Eisenhower nor Congress became involved in the race issue until 1957, when the governor of Arkansas, Orval Eugene Faubus, used the National Guard to prevent the admission of nine black students to an all-white high school in Little Rock. The confrontation in Little Rock drew international attention to racism and civil rights in the United States as well as to the battle between federal and state power. Television and newspaper reporters devoted substantial coverage to the "Little Rock Nine," as the students were called.

The Little Rock Nine

The Little Rock Nine was a group of African American high-school students who challenged racial segregation in the public schools of Little Rock, Arkansas. The group—consisting of Melba Pattillo, Ernest Green, Elizabeth Eckford, Minnijean Brown, Terrence Roberts, Carlotta Walls, Jefferson Thomas, Gloria Ray, and Thelma Mothershed—became the center of the struggle to desegregate public schools in the United States, especially in the South. The events that followed their enrollment in Little Rock Central High School provoked intense national debate about racial segregation and civil rights.

A large white mob threatened the students on their first day of school, while the Arkansas National Guard

continued on the next page

The Little Rock Nine are escorted to school by federal troops on September 25, 1957.

continued from the previous page

blocked the doors. The students stayed home for more than two weeks while President Eisenhower negotiated with Governor Faubus. Their return on September 23 was again disrupted by violent white protesters, but they were able to attend school safely two days later, protected by U.S. soldiers sent in by Eisenhower.

The Little Rock Nine continued to face physical and verbal attacks from white students throughout their studies at Central High. One of the students, Minnijean Brown, fought back and was expelled. The remaining eight students, however, attended the school for the rest of the academic year. At the end of the year, in 1958, senior Ernest Green became the first African American to graduate from Little Rock Central High School.

Governor Faubus was reelected in 1958, and rather than permit desegregation, he closed all of Little Rock's schools. Many school districts in the South followed Little Rock's example, closing schools or implementing "school-choice" programs that subsidized white students' attendance at private segregated academies, which were not covered by the Supreme Court's decision. Little Rock Central High School did not reopen with a desegregated student body until 1960, and efforts to integrate schools and other public areas throughout the country continued through the 1960s.

The president tried to settle the problem through negotiation with Governor Faubus and Little Rock's mayor, Woodrow Mann. Despite Eisenhower's publicly stated reluctance to use federal troops to enforce desegregation, he recognized the potential for violence and state insubordination. He thus sent the elite 101st Airborne Division, called the "Screaming Eagles," to Little Rock and placed the Arkansas National Guard under federal command.

In the same year Congress passed the Eisenhower Administration's civil rights bill. This was the first such bill passed in 82 years. It created a civil rights commission within the Department of Justice. It also gave the federal government authority to act in support of the Supreme Court's ban on school segregation.

Economic Recession

The Eisenhower years can, in general, be characterized as a period of growth and prosperity. Some economic problems did arise during his second term, however. In 1957–58 a recession hit and unemployment rose to its highest level since 1941. Labor problems increased in intensity, with some 500,000 steelworkers going on strike for 116 days in 1959. Industrial production declined, while consumer prices rose to record levels.

Major tax cuts were considered, but Eisenhower refused to lower taxes because he feared it could fuel inflation. The government did furnish funds to the states for those whose unemployment compensation had run out. By July 1958 government economists said the country was recovering from its worst recession since the end of World War II.

Throughout the recession the president remained personally popular. The

Congressional elections of 1958, however, reflected public discontent, with the Democrats gaining large majorities in both houses.

Peace Efforts

Eisenhower continued to emphasize the achievement of world peace as one of the prime objectives of his administration's foreign policy. Following the death of Secretary of State John Foster Dulles in 1959, the president assumed a more vigorous and personal role in foreign policy. He undertook a series of goodwill tours, traveling more than 300,000 miles (480,000 kilometers) to some 27 countries during his last two years in office.

To improve relations with the Soviet Union, Eisenhower invited Soviet Premier Nikita Khrushchev to visit the United States. Khrushchev toured parts of the country in September 1959 and held private

senhower *(left)* with Arturo Frondizi, president Argentina, in 1960.

talks with Eisenhower at Camp David, Maryland. They agreed that outstanding issues between countries should be handled by peaceful means and that general disarmament was the most important question of the day. Eisenhower was invited to pay a state visit to the Soviet Union the following year.

In December 1959 Eisenhower made a 19-day goodwill tour of 11 countries in Europe, Africa, the Middle East, and Asia. Two months later he embarked on a tour of South America. He delivered six major speeches and was enthusiastically cheered by more than 3 million people. At the conclusion of his tour, on March 7, he renewed the U.S. pledge first contained in the Rio de Janeiro Treaty of 1947, which called for mutual defense of the Americas.

In the meantime, plans for an East-West summit conference in Paris had been completed. The participants were to include President Eisenhower, Soviet Premier Khrushchev, British Prime Minister Harold Macmillan, and French President Charles de Gaulle. Among the major issues on the agenda were the problems of Germany and world disarmament.

A new era of personal diplomacy seemed at hand. On May 1, 1960, however, the Soviets shot down an American U-2 observation plane deep inside the Soviet Union. Its pilot, Gary Frances Powers, was imprisoned by the Soviets, who accused him of being a spy. Khrushchev bitterly attacked

The Soviets displayed the wreckage of the American U-2 observation plane shot down on May 1, 1960.

the United States and Eisenhower, calling the incident "aggressive provocation aimed at wrecking the summit conference."

Eisenhower's announcement that all flights over Soviet territory had been canceled failed to appease the Soviet premier. At the opening session of the Paris summit meeting on May 16, the belligerent attitude of Khrushchev wrecked any hope of continuing the conference. The Soviet leader also withdrew his invitation to President Eisenhower to visit the Soviet Union in June. Eisenhower admitted that the flights had gone on for four years and accepted much of the blame for the ill-timed incident.

Despite the collapse of the summit meeting, the president continued his policy of personal diplomacy. In June 1960 he again went abroad. On this tour he visited Alaska, the Philippines, Taiwan, Okinawa, South Korea, and Hawaii. A scheduled stop in Tokyo was canceled, however. The Japanese capital had been the scene of a series of riots protesting the proposed ratification of a new U.S.-Japan mutual security treaty. The pro-Western government of Japanese Prime Minister Nobusuke Kishi admitted that it was unable to guarantee the president's safety. The treaty, however, was ratified by the Japanese legislature on June 19, 1960.

A further display of Cold War tensions came during the last weeks of the Eisenhower Administration, when the United States broke diplomatic relations with Cuba in January 1961. For two years the country had been led by the communist regime of Fidel Castro.

Other Domestic Events

Eisenhower filled the vacancies of three retiring Supreme Court appointments during his second term. In 1957 William J. Brennan, Jr., replaced Sherman Minton, and Charles E. Whittaker succeeded Stanley F. Reed. In 1958 Eisenhower chose Potter Stewart to replace Harold H. Burton.

Two new states joined the Union during Eisenhower's presidency. In June 1958 final Congressional approval was given to making Alaska the 49th state. The president, who had urged its passage, signed the Alaska statehood bill in July. Alaska officially became a state in

Eisenhower at a celebration of statehood for Alaska and Hawaii on April 13, 1959.

January 1959. In March 1959 Congress approved statehood for Hawaii. The president signed the statehood bill in March and Hawaii was admitted to the Union in August as the 50th state.

In the final months of his administration Eisenhower sought to hold down inflation. He checked spending by Congress and by bureau and department heads in a drive to balance the budget.

FAREWELL ADDRESS

John F. Kennedy, a Democrat, was elected Eisenhower's successor in 1960. Although his presidency had a great many critics,

Eisenhower's Farewell Address was broadcast on both television and radio on January 17, 1961.

Eisenhower was still extraordinarily popular when he left office in January 1961. In his Farewell Address he warned against the rise and power of "the military-industrial complex"—the network of individuals and institutions involved in the production of weapons and military technologies. Eisenhower believed that the military-industrial complex tended to promote policies that might not be in the country's best interest, such as participation in the nuclear arms race. He feared that its growing influence, if left unchecked, could undermine American democracy. However, his successors ignored him amid the perceived national-security demands of the Cold War.

Conclusion

When Eisenhower left office, Congress restored his rank as general of the Army. He returned to his farm in Gettysburg, Pennsylvania, and devoted much of his time to writing his memoirs. In 1963 he published *Mandate for Change*, which was followed in 1965 by *Waging Peace*. A lighter work, *At Ease: Stories I Tell to Friends,* appeared in 1967. In 1962 he dedicated the Eisenhower Presidential Library in Abilene, Kansas, which houses the bulk of his personal and state papers.

After a long period of illness and a hospital confinement of almost a year, Eisenhower died of heart failure on March 28, 1969, at the Walter Reed General Hospital in Washington. A three-day state funeral was held in Washington, after which Eisenhower was buried in Abilene in the chapel at the Eisenhower Center.

The Eisenhower Presidential Library and Museum is located in the former president's childhood hometown of Abilene, Kansas.

Glossary

amphibious Executed by coordinated action of land, sea, and air forces organized for invasion from the sea, usually employing warships, assault boats, landing barges, assault troops, aircraft carriers, and covering aircraft.

armada A fleet of warships, or a large force of other vehicles such as planes.

belligerent Exhibiting hostility or combativeness.

blacklist A list of persons who are disapproved of or are to be punished or discriminated against.

censure To officially criticize (someone or something) strongly and publicly.

communism A political and economic system in which the major productive resources in a society—such as mines, factories, and farms—are owned by the public or the state.

containment The policy or process of preventing the expansion of a hostile power or ideology.

derogatory Expressive of a low opinion of someone or something; disdainful.

diphtheria A highly contagious disease that is marked by the formation of a false membrane especially in the throat. It is caused by a bacterium that produces a toxin causing inflammation of the heart and nervous system.

disarmament The reduction and limitation of weaponry.

excise tax A sales tax on a specific type of commodity, such as alcohol, tobacco, or automobiles.

garrison A body of troops stationed at a military stronghold.

hydrogen bomb A bomb that produces an extremely powerful and destructive explosion when hydrogen atoms unite.

ideological Of, relating to, or based on the set of ideas and beliefs of a group or political party.

inflation A continuing rise in the general price level usually attributed to an increase in the volume of money and credit relative to available goods.

insubordination Defiance of authority.

intercontinental ballistic missile A land-based, nuclear-armed, rocket-propelled guided weapon with a range of more than 3,500 miles (5,600 kilometers).

McCarthyism The persecution of innocent people using powerful but unproved allegations. It refers to U.S. Senator Joseph McCarthy's charges of communist subversion and high treason in the U.S. federal government in the 1950s.

nullify To make legally null and void; cancel.

transcontinental Extending or going across a continent.

unchecked Not curbed or hindered; unrestricted.

unconstitutional Not allowed by the constitution of a country of government; specifically, contrary to the U.S. Constitution.

For More Information

Dwight D. Eisenhower Presidential Library, Museum and Boyhood Home
200 Southeast Fourth Street
Abilene, KS 67410
(785) 263-6700
Website: http://www.eisenhower.archives.gov
This institution is administered by the National Archives and Records Administration and hosts a wealth of information on Eisenhower, his presidency, and the times he lived in. Many documents and photographs are available online, with additional films and artifacts on display at the library in Abilene, Kansas.

Federal Highway Administration (FHWA)
1200 New Jersey Avenue SE

Washington, DC 20590
(202) 366-4000
Website: https://www.fhwa.dot.gov
Part of the U.S. Department of Transportation, the FHWA oversees the construction and maintenance of highways, bridges, and tunnels, including the Interstate Highway System launched by Eisenhower in 1956. The FHWA was created in 1966, although other organizations had supported American roads before that.

The Miller Center
P.O. Box 400406
Charlottesville, VA 22904
(434) 924-7236
Website: http://millercenter.org
The Miller Center, based at the University of Virginia, is a nonpartisan research facility focused on the history of the U.S. presidency. One of the center's ongoing projects is to transcribe the secret White House recordings of presidents Franklin D. Roosevelt, Harry S. Truman, Dwight D. Eisenhower, John F. Kennedy, Lyndon B. Johnson, and Richard Nixon.

National Aeronautics and Space Administration (NASA)
300 E. Street SW, Suite 5R30
Washington, DC 20546
(202) 358-0001
Website: https://www.nasa.gov
NASA was established in 1958, during Dwight D. Eisenhower's presidency, in response to the Soviet Union's successful launch of Sputnik the year before. Eleven years after its creation, NASA succeeded in sending a manned mission to the Moon. Its unmanned programs have explored the planets and other bodies in the solar system.

National Association for the Advancement of Colored People (NAACP)
4805 Mt. Hope Drive
Baltimore, MD 21215
(410) 580-5777
Website: http://www.naacp.org
Founded in 1909, the NAACP aims to eliminate discrimination and achieve equality between people of all races. One of the first major victories of its Legal Defense and Education Fund was the 1954 Supreme Court case *Brown* v.

Board of Education of Topeka, which outlawed school segregation.

National D-Day Memorial
P.O. Box 77
Bedford, VA 24523
(800) 351-DDAY
Website: https://www.dday.org
The National D-Day Memorial holds events and educational programs commemorating the Normandy Invasion of World War II.

National Museum of American History
14th Street and Constitution Avenue NW
Washington, DC 20001
(202) 633-1000
Website: http://americanhistory.si.edu/presidency
One of the ongoing exhibits at the Smithsonian's National Museum of American History is entitled "The American Presidency: A Glorious Burden," which examines how American presidents have impacted history.

North Atlantic Treaty Organization (NATO)
Boulevard Leopold III

1110 Brussels
Belgium
Website: http://www.nato.int
NATO is a political and military alliance comprising the United States, Canada, and numerous European countries. Originally formed as a protection against the communist bloc in eastern Europe after World War II, NATO is now concerned with general defense and security issues.

Websites

Because of the changing nature of Internet links, Rosen Publishing has developed an online list of websites related to the subject of this book. This site is updated regularly. Please use this link to access the list:

http://www.rosenlinks.com/PPPL/eisen

For Further Reading

Feinstein, Stephen. *The 1950s* (Decades of the 20th and 21st Centuries). New York, NY: Enslow Publishing, 2016.

George, Enzo. *The Cold War* (Primary Sources in U.S. History). New York, NY: Cavendish Square, 2016.

Haskew, Michael E. *West Point 1915: Eisenhower, Bradley, and the Class the Stars Fell On*. Minneapolis, MN: Zenith Press, 2014.

Johnson, Paul. *Eisenhower: A Life.* New York, NY: Viking Books, 2014.

Klein, Rebecca T. *School Integration: Brown v. Board of Education of Topeka* (A Celebration of the Civil Rights Movement). New York, NY: Rosen Publishing, 2015.

Kling, Andrew A. *The Red Scare* (World History). San Diego, CA: Lucent Books, 2011.

Krumm, Brian. *The Little Rock Nine: A Primary Source Exploration of the Battle for School*

Integration (We Shall Overcome). North Mankato, MN: Capstone Publishing, 2014.

Lindop, Edmund, with Sarah DeCapua. *America in the 1950s* (The Decades of Twentieth-Century America). Minneapolis, MN: Twenty-First Century Books, 2010.

Mayer, Michael S. *The Eisenhower Years* (Presidential Profiles). New York, NY: Facts on File, 2010.

Murphy, John. *The Eisenhower Interstate System* (Building America: Then and Now). New York, NY: Chelsea House Publishers, 2009.

Newton, Jim. *Eisenhower: The White House Years*. New York, NY: Anchor, 2012.

Nichols, David A. *Eisenhower 1956: The President's Year of Crisis—Suez and the Brink of War.* New York, NY: Simon & Schuster, 2012.

Sambaluk, Nicholas Michael. *The Other Space Race: Eisenhower and the Quest for Aerospace Security.* Annapolis, MD: Naval Institute Press, 2015.

Index

A

B

C

D

E